Speedway Superstars

written by James Buckley, Jr.

Reader's Digest
Children's Books™

Pleasantville, New York • Montréal, Québec • Bath, United Kingdom

Published by Reader's Digest Children's Books
Reader's Digest Road, Pleasantville, NY U.S.A. 10570-7000
and Reader's Digest Children's Publishing Limited,
The Ice House, 124-126 Walcot Street, Bath UK BA1 5BG
Reader's Digest Children's Books is a trademark
and Reader's Digest is a registered trademark
of The Reader's Digest Association, Inc.
NASCAR® is a registered trademark of the
National Association for Stock Car Auto Racing, Inc.
All rights reserved. Manufactured in China.
10 9 8 7 6 5 4 3 2 1

Manuscript and consulting services provided by
Shoreline Publishing Group LLC.

Library of Congress Cataloging-in-Publication Data

Buckley, James, 1963-.
    NASCAR : speedway superstars / written by James Buckley, Jr.
      p. cm.
  ISBN 0-7944-0406-5
  1. Stock car drivers—United States–Biography–Juvenile literature. 2. Stock car
racing—United States—Juvenile literature. 3. NASCAR (Association) [1. Automobile
racing drivers. 2. Stack car racing. 3. NASCAR (Association)] I. Title: Speedway
superstars. II. Title

  GV1032.A1B3 2004
  796.72'092'2–dc22
[B]

                          2003064942

Contents

Introduction:

Behind the Wheel

NASCAR's hottest racing machines zoom around the track. They roar down the backstretch and make a high-banked turn, and then race for the checkered flag. The cars' colorful bodies are just inches away from each other as they race at 150 miles per hour. The fans watch for the numbers of their favorite drivers as the cars' engines strain for one more surge of power. The exciting spectacle climaxes as the winning car races across the finish line!

But none of this action would have happened without one important ingredient. As technologically advanced as they are, NASCAR's automobiles can't go anywhere without one vital part: the driver!

The men behind the machines are the real heroes of NASCAR, not their high-tech machines. The drivers combine bravery, talent, and technique to guide their 3,400-pound monsters through each hot, grueling race.

"Driving a race car in a 500-mile race is a real test of a man's strength and stamina," says Richard "The King" Petty, NASCAR's most successful driver ever (see chapter 2). "The race is a three-and-a-half hour ordeal with no time-outs or rest periods."

With the wind whipping their faces, the steering wheel vibrating in their hands, and the lure of Victory Lane ahead, NASCAR drivers have only one goal: Win.

The road to becoming a NASCAR driver, and getting into position to win, is a long and hard one. Drivers spend long hours in the seats of all sorts of racing machines, from mini-cars and karts to trucks and stock cars. They learn constantly, studying other racers, and tinkering with their cars to learn what makes them work. Drivers practice with their pit crews to be swift and sure during all-important pit stops. Like other athletes, NASCAR drivers work just as hard during the race week as they do on race day.

After years on the smaller tracks, the best of them wind up in NASCAR's top division, racing every weekend before millions of fans watching either in person or on TV. The best of these select few wind up in front of the pack more than others.

As the racers are called to the track, they slide in through the car windows. (There are no doors on

NASCAR cars!) They strap themselves into their seats, which are specially molded for each driver. Strapping on their helmets and plugging in their radio earpieces, they are ready to race. The anticipation might make them breathless or excited, or they might be calm and collected. This is the moment they've waited and worked for. When that green flag drops, they'll be doing something they love more than anything in the world: racing to win!

Over the next few hours, they'll be in that seat without a single second of rest or relaxation. A moment's distraction could mean disaster or defeat. But this is the life they have chosen, the life they love. And when one racer finally zooms under that checkered flag, and, moments later, climbs out amid the cheers on Victory Lane, he'll know he has earned a new title, one even better than "driver."

He has become a "winner."

This book celebrates the men who drive the cars, the heroes whose talents thrill millions every weekend that NASCAR races. Some drivers are tough, some are crafty, but there is one thing they all are—fast!

On the Beach

Some of the first stock car races were not held on asphalt or dirt. They were held on sand! In Daytona Beach, Florida, there are long, wide stretches of hard-packed sand along the shoreline. Driving souped-up passenger cars, racers drove on a long oval course, half of which was on the sand. The other half was on a road that ran parallel to the beach.

At each end of the loop were tight turns. In those days, drivers did not have the advantage of "power steering." Power steering helps make steering today's cars very easy. Instead, drivers often had to use muscle power to turn their steering wheels and aim their heavy machines around the turns. Fans stood in tightly packed crowds along the edges of the course. Sometimes they were only a few feet from the cars.

The cars had to be powerful, but not just for gaining speed in the straightaways. In the turns, they had to churn through softer, mushier sand. As the races went on, the sand became more and more churned up. Cars sometimes skidded sideways or became stuck in deep sand. Racing on the beach was a far cry from today's stock car speedways, but it was a great place for the sport to start!

Chapter 1

Pioneers of Speed

The first stock car drivers didn't have far to go to reach their racing machines. Often, all they had to do was open the door to the family garage! The first stock car racers didn't race for a living, they raced as more of a hobby. On small tracks in the South, in states such as Florida, Georgia, and North Carolina, they took the family cars out to race against fellow drivers. It was not unusual for a driver to go from home to the track. They'd drive in a race and drive the same car back home. You can't do that with today's NASCAR speed machines!

Stock car drivers in those days—the years before and after World War II (1941–45)—all had regular jobs. Some were businessmen or worked in stores or factories. Most, however, worked around cars for a living as mechanics, garage owners, or car salesmen. Racing, for them, didn't pay the bills, but it was what they lived for.

By the middle of the 1940s, there were so many different races at tracks all over the country, it was hard to keep them all straight. Certain races were held some years, and not held other years. The organizers of some races were not completely honest, and some drivers got cheated. The time had come for stock car drivers to get organized.

Some of the most famous and successful races in those days were held on the hard-packed sand of Daytona Beach, Florida. It was there that a driver and car owner named Bill France got all the drivers together at a meeting in late 1947. It was time to go from rough-and-tumble to safe and professional. In early 1948, the drivers, led by France, dropped the checkered flag on a new organization: the National Association for Stock Car Automobile Racing, NASCAR for short.

NASCAR was a dream come true for "Big Bill," and the nation's best drivers flocked to the new series of races. They kept their regular jobs, but now they could earn some good money by winning rough-and-tumble races. The new organization inspired others to build better and larger tracks to hold the growing crowds clamoring to see these hot wheels. In addition, NASCAR created a series of races that would lead to an annual series championship. Drivers would earn points for how they finished in each race. The driver with the most points would be the champ. This system is pretty much the same today.

Facilities improved, too. Darlington Speedway was built in 1950 as the first of the "superspeedways." In 1959, the France family finished construction on the 2.5-mile-long Daytona International Speedway, which would become the home of the Super Bowl of NASCAR racing, the Daytona 500. As tracks improved and crowds grew, drivers began to enjoy the benefits of better cars and more help. Instead of getting new pit crews for each race assembled from local mechanics, drivers began to work with regular team members. Sponsors began to see the appeal of these races to fans, and their support helped increase prize money to drivers and helped the new sport grow.

But with all these improvements, the races still came down to which man could drive his car faster than all the others. Many top drivers from those days remain among NASCAR's most legendary stars. Some of the best from this early era included:

Lee Petty
The father of Richard Petty (see chapter 2), Lee won three NASCAR season titles in the 1950s

Racing on the beach in Daytona

(1954, '58, and '59). In 1959, Lee also was the first winner of what would become the world's most famous stock car race: The Daytona 500. His record of 54 race victories was an all-time best, until his son overtook him in 1967.

Tim Flock

The 1952 and 1955 NASCAR champion, Tim was part of a famous racing family. His brothers Fonty and Bob raced, as did their sister Ethel. In 1955, Tim set a record by winning 18 races (later broken by Richard Petty's 27 in 1967) and 19 pole positions (a mark that still stands). Tim was also famous for having included his pet monkey Jocko as a "copilot" early in his career.

Junior Johnson

Charging out of the hills of North Carolina, Junior was a success on and off the track. As a driver, he won 50 races from 1953 to 1966. As a car owner, his teams won six titles in NASCAR's top division. In 1963, he drove a car that won or finished second 17 times, but didn't finish any other races because the engine failed. "We just drove that car to go or blow," he was famous for saying.

Buck Baker

This former bus driver was the first to win

NASCAR's season series twice (1956 and 1957). Buck was one of the most versatile drivers ever, with success at every level of stock car racing.

Ned Jarrett

Though recent NASCAR fans probably are more familiar with Ned's work as a TV announcer, he was one of early NASCAR's top drivers. He won the series title in 1961 and 1965, along with 50 career race victories. Ned's son, Dale, was the 1999 series champion, joining the Pettys as the only father-and-son NASCAR champs.

These and other early pioneers set the stage for the growth of NASCAR. Their bravery and driving skills were the models for all the drivers who would come after them.

It's All Relative

The France family has remained in the leadership of NASCAR. Bill Sr. was followed by his son Bill Jr. who recently passed the reins to his son Brian, "Big Bill's" grandson. Family continues to be a big part of NASCAR tradition. Here is a partial list of some of the generations of great NASCAR drivers.

Fathers and Sons

Lee and Richard Petty

Richard and Kyle and Adam Petty

Ned and Dale Jarrett

Buck and Buddy Baker

Dale and Dale Earnhardt Jr.

Bobby and Davey and Clifford Allison

Brothers

Tim, Fonty, and Bob Flock (plus sister Ethel)

Terry and Bobby Labonte

Bobby and Donnie Allison

Darrell and Michael Waltrip

Rusty, Mike, and Kenny Wallace

Geoff, Brett, and Todd Bodine

Jeff and Ward Burton

Chapter 2

The King

If NASCAR racing has a Babe Ruth, it has to be
Richard Petty. No other driver in the history of the
sport has won more races, more annual championships,
more Daytona 500s, and more respect than the driver
they call "The King." Petty's long, successful career
helped NASCAR turn from a small, Southern series of
races into an international spectacle. Along the way,
Petty himself remained the down-home, good-natured
speed demon he was from his childhood.

The future King was born in North Carolina in
1937. His father, Lee, drove a truck for a living, but what
Lee really loved to do was race stock cars. Richard
grew up with engine grease under his fingernails. He
had a wrench in his hand from the time he was strong
enough to carry one. While he grew up to be a great
all-around athlete in high school, engines, cars, and
speed were his real passions.

Lee started racing in the late 1940s, about when

NASCAR was born. He started racing at age 35! He learned fast though.

Richard and his brother Maurice helped Lee prepare his cars for racing. By 1948, when NASCAR was born, Lee was one of the best drivers around. The Petty family followed Lee around the South to small dirt tracks every weekend. Richard watched excitedly from the stands or from pit row as his dad zoomed around the track, often ending up in Victory Lane.

Richard wanted to follow in his father's tire tracks and race in NASCAR. But Lee knew that being a driver was a tough job, one that would take skill and determination. He made Richard wait until he was 21 years old before he allowed him to race. On July 12, 1958, just days after his 21st birthday, Richard Petty started the greatest career in NASCAR history in a small race in North Carolina. He started fast and didn't look back for more than 34 years.

Over the rest of that first year, Richard improved with every race. His car bore the number 43, in honor of his dad's car number 42. In 1959, Lee helped make NASCAR history, too, by winning the very first Daytona 500. The famous Daytona International Speedway had just opened, and Lee barely nosed out Johnny Beauchamp for the victory in what would become NASCAR's most storied annual event.

Lee ended his career in 1964 with three NASCAR championships and 54 race victories, both all-time records until his son came along to break them.

Meanwhile, Richard had enough high finishes to earn the 1959 NASCAR rookie of the year award. Over the next several years, almost every NASCAR season would find Richard adding another milestone to his career...and his life:

- 1960: After finishing third in the Daytona 500, Richard won his first NASCAR race, a 100-mile event in Charlotte, North Carolina.

- 1962: Richard won nine races and finished second overall, behind Joe Weatherly.

- 1963: Although he had 14 wins on the year, Richard again was number-two behind Weatherly.

- 1964: Richard won his first Daytona 500, setting a track record with an average speed of more than 154 miles per hour. He also won his first NASCAR points championship in what was then known as the Grand National.

In 1965, the Petty racing team faced some controversy. Richard's No. 43 car had been using a Chrysler "hemi" engine. It was a newer, more powerful engine than some drivers had. NASCAR ruled that he couldn't use the engine that season, and Richard sat out the first half of the racing season in protest. NASCAR soon changed its mind, however, and Richard won five of the 14 races he was in that year.

The 1966 season began with another victory at the Daytona 500, with Petty setting another track record. He would finish the season with eight more victories, good for third overall in the points standings.

Richard had put a lot of miles on his No. 43 car and carried home many checkered flags in his short time in NASCAR. His hard-charging style and ready smile made him a fan favorite, too; he would be voted the Most Popular Driver nine times by the fans. With two Daytonas and a series title under his belt, he was among the circuit's most successful drivers. But no one, not even his greatest fans, could have predicted what he would do in the 1967 season.

He started out slowly, with a poor finish at Daytona. But soon he began the most amazing season in motor sports history. Before the final checkered flag fell in November, Richard Petty won an astonishing 27 races (out of a total of 48 run that year). Included in that huge total were 10 victories in a row, beginning in August and ending in Wilkesboro, North Carolina, in October.

Richard Petty

With his sixth victory of that year, Richard also became NASCAR's all-time leader in victories, topping his father's total of 54. Not surprisingly, Richard also won the NASCAR championship that season, this time by the widest margin in the sport's history. (That record that still stands, like his total of 27 wins and streak of 10).

That 1967 season put Petty on an even higher level than he had been before. It was the year that he earned his famous nickname, "The King."

"I'm not saying I'm the best driver or that I have the best pit crew," he said at the time. "But I believe we have the best combination. We've been lucky… you have to be lucky to win 10 straight."

Helping keep The King down-to-earth was his "queen," Lynda, whom he had married in 1959. They had one son, Kyle, who would follow in the family business as a top driver. The Pettys also have three daughters, Sharon, Lisa, and Rebecca.

As Petty's family, reputation, and winnings grew, so did NASCAR. Through the 1960s, NASCAR was not very well-known outside of the South and its devoted fans. Petty's success was so enormous that a wider audience began to track this high-speed, hot-action sport. In the early 1970s, more races began to be on television, helping millions more people appreciate the skill and style of the drivers. As the best driver on the track, Petty led the way there, too.

Another way he led the pack was in the area of sponsorship. In 1972, he signed with the STP company, which made various engine-care products. The STP logo appeared on all of Petty's cars and uniforms, while the money the company brought in helped Petty stay on top of the competition.

The 1970s belonged to No. 43. Petty won five driving titles, bringing his career total to seven. Only the great Dale Earnhardt (see chapter 4) has matched that total, and only Jeff Gordon, with four, has come close. In the 1970s, Richard also won four Daytona 500s and dozens of other races. His smiling face, under his famous cowboy hat with big feathered brim, became the sport's most recognizable symbol.

In 1981, Richard won his seventh and final Daytona 500. Though he was still among the top drivers, he began to win less often. On July 4, 1984, at the Firecracker 500 at Daytona, Richard won his 200th race. It was his final victory in a NASCAR race, but that career total remains an untouchable record. Only one other driver, David Pearson with 105 wins, has even half as many as Richard Petty.

Richard kept racing for several more seasons, but the competition was catching up to him. It was time to leave the driver's seat for the last time. In 1992, fans saluted him at each stop on the circuit during the "Richard Petty Fan Appreciation Tour."

Many honors would come his way after he left the track. In 1992, he was awarded the United States Medal of Freedom, the highest award given to American civilians. He was named the Man of the Year by an automotive writers' group for his contributions to the community in 1995. And he was named to the International Motorsports Hall of Fame in 1997.

But just because the King was no longer behind the wheel, that didn't mean he wasn't still prowling the track. Petty Enterprises, the company founded by Lee and continued by Richard, remains a force in NASCAR. In 2003, Kyle Petty and Christian Fittipaldi drove Petty Enterprises cars, with Richard directing operations. For Richard Petty, being out in front remains the goal. Only these days, he's doing it not behind the wheel, but behind the scenes.

"One of these days," said Petty, "when they have a race and I don't show up, then everybody will know I've retired."

Petty's Kingdom

Richard Petty was the points champion of NASCAR's top series in each of the following years:

1964 1967 1971 1972
1974 1975 1979

He finished second in these years:

1962 1963 1969 1976 1977

By the Numbers

Fans love stats, so here are some numbers to consider. All of these are all-time NASCAR records:

Wins:	200
Top five finishes:	555
Top ten finishes:	712
Pole positions:	126
Races started:	1,184
Laps led:	52,194
Laps completed:	307,836

The Ultimate Rivalry

While Richard Petty was certainly the King of NASCAR in the 1960s and 1970s, there were many rivals for his crown. One of the most successful was David Pearson. For more than 15 years, Petty vs. Pearson became one of the most heated rivalries in sports. The two ace drivers finished 1–2 in 63 races, with Pearson having a three-victory edge.

Pearson, also from North Carolina, would have been the sport's best driver if it weren't for Petty. Pearson was the NASCAR champion in 1966, 1968, and 1969. He did not have Petty's outgoing personality, but was nearly the King's equal on the track. His 105 victories are the second-highest total in NASCAR history.

At the 1976 Daytona 500, this fearsome rivalry had its most famous clash. As the race neared the end, the two were neck and neck on the final lap. Petty had a slight lead, then Pearson gunned his engine and passed the King. On the last turn, Petty tried to get the lead back and the two cars crashed. Both machines spun into the infield, their front ends smashed. However, Pearson managed to restart his car and rolled slowly across the finish line to win, while Petty fumed in his broken car.

It was a smoking end to a fiery rivalry.

82

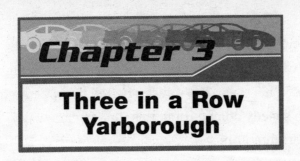

Chapter 3

Three in a Row Yarborough

From 1974 through 1979, only two men won NASCAR's season championship. One was the famous "King," Richard Petty. The other was a hard-working South Carolina native who had been so eager to start racing that he had lied about his age so that he could jump behind the wheel of a stock car when he was only 18. Cale Yarborough went from that youthful fib to one of the greatest careers in NASCAR history, winning 83 races and becoming, from 1976–78, the only driver ever to capture three straight season championships.

Cale's road to those titles began at the top of a hill in Timmonsville, South Carolina. His passion as a youngster was soap box derby, a kind of racing in which youngsters drive homemade cars down hills. The only power they use is gravity, so creating a car that moves through the air quickly is important. Young Cale was thrilled by the speed and the wind whipping through his hair as he rolled down the hill, side-by-side with other boys' cars. Cale never won the big races in his town, but it just whetted his appetite for more speedy competition, this time in cars with powerful motors.

In high school, he also competed in football, helping his team advance to the state finals. He was named all-state for his performance as running back. He was also a state champion boxer in the Golden Gloves competition. Doing his best to win became a hallmark of everything Cale did, on the track, in the ring, or in life.

Wanting to test his racing skills at the highest level, Cale needed a NASCAR license. However, at the time, a driver had to be 21 to earn a ride in that big-time series, and Cale was only 18 in 1957. He got some help from a friend in the courthouse in town and got a certificate to send to NASCAR saying he was 21. Well, he didn't get away with it, at least not entirely. NASCAR officials at Darlington Raceway for the Southern 500 saw through his ruse and kicked him out of the car...several times! Cale was persistent, however, and ended up driving several laps during the race. But it would be four more years until he got back in a NASCAR race. Of course, once he was in for good, he was determined to reach the top.

Cale's first five seasons in NASCAR weren't too successful, however. He struggled to keep his spot on the racing team, and he didn't put up too many good finishes. But that youthful persistence kept him going. In 1966, he joined the team run by the famous Wood brothers, who had worked on perfecting the art of the pit stop, among other innovations. With the Woods, Cale soared. In 1967, he won his first superspeedway race at Atlanta, and the next year he won the Daytona 500 and five other races. In 1968, he finally won at the track he called "home" in Darlington, not far from his birthplace. In fact, Cale went on to win five Southern 500s at that famous track, more than any other driver.

By the mid-1970s, Cale's experience and the expertise of his new team leader, Junior Johnson, put Cale among NASCAR's best. He finished second to Benny Parsons in the 1973 rankings and trailed only Richard Petty in 1974. He also won Southern 500 races both years as well. He also kept up his winning ways at the Bristol Motor Speedway in Tennessee, where he won an all-time record nine races in his career.

In 1976, Cale put it all together and began his remarkable string of three straight NASCAR championships. In 1977, he finished in the top 10 in 27 of 30 races. Another highlight of those years was his second Daytona 500 victory in 1977.

Even though Cale was now the best stock car driver in the world, he was still the good ol' boy from South Carolina. In his autobiography, *Cale* (written with William Neely), he tells the story of putting on his old hunting overalls after one winning season. They were worn and beat-up and falling apart. "I told my buddies that if I won again at Daytona, I'm gonna get me a new pair of overalls." But, he writes, even after winning ten different races at Daytona, Cale never replaced those comfortable old clothes.

Cale capped off his great career with two more Daytona 500 victories in 1983 and 1984. He retired in 1988 with 83 race victories, now good for fifth best all-time.

From a "false start" as a teenager to a fourth Daytona win at the age of 44, Cale had made it not to the bottom of a hill...but to the top!

Cale Yarborough

Owners and Sponsors

In 1976, Cale Yarborough drove an orange-and-yellow Chevy Monte Carlo to his first of three straight NASCAR championships. The car was sponsored by Holly Farms, a food company. The sponsorship of race cars became a big part of the sport in the early 1960s and boomed in the 1970s as NASCAR races appeared on television more and more. Companies knew that consumers who saw their product names on race cars and on drivers' suits might decide to buy those products, especially if their favorite driver won a lot of races.

Sponsors generally do not "own" the cars; race teams spend the money to buy and maintain the cars for their teams. However, the sponsors' money plays a big part in helping teams maintain their operations. Some sponsors become part of all teams by signing up with NASCAR's headquarters. But every team has numerous sponsors, big and small, of its own. Generally, one major sponsor gets its name on the hood of the car and prominently on the drivers' gear. Jeff Gordon drives a DuPont Chevrolet, for instance, while Matt Kenseth is in the DeWalt Tools car, and Tony Stewart drives The Home Depot car.

Keeping Track at the Track

Stock car racers have always put numbers on their cars, usually to help fans and judges identify each vehicle. Unlike some sports, NASCAR numbers are not "retired." So you see that legends of the past, such as Ned Jarrett and Cale Yarborough, shared No. 11 with more recent star Darrell Waltrip. Bobby Allison, a top driver in the '70s and '80s, and current driver Michael Waltrip both drove the No. 15 car. However, many drivers are well-known by the numbers they used for the bulk of their careers. Here are some of the most well-known numbers in NASCAR and the drivers who helped make them famous.

2	Rusty Wallace	**17**	Darrell Waltrip
3	Dale Earnhardt Sr.		Matt Kenseth
	Junior Johnson	**18**	Bobby Labonte
5	Terry Labonte	**20**	Tony Stewart
6	Mark Martin	**21**	David Pearson
8	Dale Earnhardt Jr.	**23**	Bobby Allison
9	Bill Elliott	**24**	Jeff Gordon
11	Darrell Waltrip	**40**	Sterling Marlin
	Cale Yarborough	**42**	Lee Petty
	Ned Jarrett	**43**	Richard Petty
12	Ryan Newman	**48**	Jimmie Johnson
	Joe Weatherly	**88**	Dale Jarrett
15	Buddy Baker	**99**	Jeff Burton
	Michael Waltrip		

Chapter 4

The Man in Black

Few NASCAR drivers have been as beloved by fans and respected by opponents as Dale Earnhardt Sr. The fabled "Man in Black," named for his No. 3 car's black paint, is one of the top drivers of all time, with a record seven season championships. He also racked up more than $41 million in career earnings, more than any other driver. Throughout his career, he was known for one thing: heading for the front and never letting anything get in this way.

Earnhardt was following in his father's footsteps. Ralph Earnhardt was one of the top stock car drivers of the 1950s and 1960s, winning more than 500 races of various types. Ralph was so good that he was inducted into the International Motorsports Hall of Fame in 1989.

"I think I watched every foot of every lap he ever ran after I started going to races with him," said Dale in 1990. "And I was almost always at his elbow in the garage or the backyard, trying to see what made his cars so strong."

Dale started racing when he was a teenager, working his way up to NASCAR's top level by 1975, when he was only 24 years old. He raced there part-time for several years, and in 1979, moved up to the "big league" full time. It was a good move. Dale won his first race (the Southeastern 500 in Bristol, Tennessee) in only his sixteenth pro start. He added 10 more top-five finishes and was named the rookie of the year.

The next year, Dale kept moving up. He won five races and became the first driver to win the rookie of the year award and the season championship in consecutive seasons. In 1981, Dale made another key move, joining car owner Richard Childress' team. Dale drove 11 races for Childress in 1981. He left the team later that year, but returned in 1984. Dale and Childress would become one of the most successful pairs in racing history.

From 1982 through 1985, the team won nine races and finished in the top 10 in points three times. The 1986 season was another breakthrough. For the second time, No. 3 was number one, winning five races and posting 16 top-five finishes. Earnhardt took the championship again in 1987, setting a career high with 11 race victories. That season, Goodwrench became Dale's sponsor, and an all-black paint scheme was put on his car. The "Man in Black" was born. Dale was third in 1988 and second in 1989.

In 1990, he was back on top again, notching nine wins and topping $3 million in earnings for the first time. He repeated as champion again in 1991. He slipped to twelfth in 1992 and then collected two more back-to-back titles. The 1994 season championship tied him with Richard Petty with seven, the most ever.

In the nine-year stretch from 1986 to 1994, Dale was in the top three each year but two, and finished first six times. It was an amazing streak of successes, and made Dale a household name and NASCAR's most famous driver.

Dale won races on superspeedways, on short tracks, on mile ovals, on road courses, just about any place NASCAR traveled. But throughout his long career, one goal eluded him: the Daytona 500, the most famous race of the year. Dale had come achingly close several times, but never captured the checkered flag in the famous race. He had won 29 other events on the famous track, but never its signature event. Finally, on his twentieth try in 1998, as both fans and

Dale Earnhardt and his car (inset)

opponents cheered, he roared to victory. After the race, the members of every team's pit crew lined up along pit road as he slowly drove down it. He reached his hand out the driver's window and slapped hands with all the crews. It was a highly charged emotional moment in a truly memorable career.

Dale remained one of the top drivers, but after his last championship in 1994, some wondered if he had the stuff to stay near the top. Were younger drivers passing him by? Would his hard-charging style still take him to the top? After all, he had earned the nickname "The Intimidator" for his ability to bull his way to victory no matter what obstacles or other drivers were in his path. "I want to give more than a hundred percent every race," he once said. "And if that's being aggressive, then I reckon I am."

In 2000, the "old man" proved that he still had the right stuff. Winning nearly $5 million, along with two races, Dale finished second behind Bobby Labonte —and ahead of young stars like Jeff Burton and Tony Stewart. No one thought he was too old then!

By the end of that season, Dale had won 76 races in his career, among the most ever in NASCAR, and more than $41 million—the most ever. At that time, his No. 3 car was the most well-known in the world of

No. 3, "The Intimidator," Dale Earnhardt

NASCAR, and Dale Earnhardt souvenirs were the most sought-after by fans. Plus, Dale had the added joy of watching his son Dale Jr. zoom into NASCAR's top ranks as one of the circuit's hottest young drivers. Dale had also started his own racing team, Dale Earnhardt International (DEI) and was helping young racers make their NASCAR dreams come true. Sadly, Dale's life and career came to an end during the 2001 Daytona 500, when he was killed in an accident.

The legacy of Dale Earnhardt will forever be a part of NASCAR history. He will be remembered as one of stock car racing's greatest champions, and an example of how to achieve the one goal every driver strives for: winning.

Daytona 500

It's appropriate that NASCAR's biggest race always comes first on the calendar. Each NASCAR season kicks off with the Daytona 500, the most famous race in the stock car world. It is held at the 2.5-mile "tri-oval" at Daytona Beach, Florida.

The Daytona International Speedway opened in 1959. The first 500 was one of the most famous, as two cars finished in a near dead-heat. It took three days for judges to study photos of the finish and declare Lee Petty as the winner.

In the years since, all of NASCAR's greatest drivers have made a mark on the Daytona stage. From NASCAR legend Junior Johnson (1960 winner) to Richard Petty (a record seven wins), from racing stars like Mario Andretti to A.J. Foyt, from hot young drivers like Jeff Gordon (only 25 when he won his first 500 in 1997) to surprises like Ward Burton in 2002, the Daytona 500 is always a place where great NASCAR memories are made.

Chapter 5

The Kid's
a Champ

Jeff Gordon was only 4 years old the first time he got behind the wheel of a miniature race car. He was only 8 when he won a national championship driving quarter-midget cars. He was 13 when he began racing 650-700 horsepower sprint cars, and 19 when he became the youngest national champion in the history of midget-car racing.

"All my life I've been pushed to do things at a young age," he says. "I always was one step ahead of the other guys."

He has stayed ahead of the pack in the "big leagues" of stock car racing, too. When Jeff was just 24 years old, he won the first of his four NASCAR season points titles. He was the youngest champion of the modern era. By the time he was 30, he had driven his trademark, multi-colored, No. 24 Chevrolet Monte Carlo to three more championships. No other driver—not even the legendary Richard Petty or the great Dale Earnhardt Sr.—who each had seven career championships—had won four NASCAR titles at such a young age.

Jeff got so good so fast on the NASCAR circuit that the media and race fans quickly took to calling him the "Wonder Boy."

"It's just a big blur, how fast I've gotten to this level," he said after he began stockpiling NASCAR championships.

The "Wonder Boy" was born in Vallejo, California, on August 4, 1971. His racing career began in youth-level races on tracks on the fairgrounds of his hometown. He had little trouble beating other children his own age, but he soon began dreaming of something bigger.

When Jeff was nine, he and his family took a trip to Indianapolis, Indiana, where they visited the Indianapolis Motor Speedway. That's the home of the Indianapolis 500, one of the most famous races in the world. Jeff visited the track the day after the big event.

"I thought it was the greatest thing!" Jeff says. "We saw where the cars actually ran, and where they went for pit stops."

He began idolizing Indianapolis 500 winners such as A.J. Foyt, Rick Mears, and Al Unser. Then, five years later, Jeff's family moved to Pittsboro, Indiana, which isn't far from Indianapolis. The local racing rules there enabled him to race bigger cars at a younger age. And soon, when he was old enough to drive on city streets, he would drive by the Indianapolis Motor Speedway. On those trips, he dreamed that one day he would take the checkered flag at the famous racetrack, which was also was known as the "Brickyard."

Little did Jeff realize that his dream soon would come true—but with a twist. Until that time, only Indy cars raced at the Brickyard. Indy cars are open-wheel, open-cockpit race cars. They are much different from NASCAR's stock cars. And until that time, Jeff had never raced a stock car. He thought he would someday race an Indy car. However, his career took a sudden and unexpected turn when he got behind the wheel of a stock car for the first time when he was 19 years old. It was at a driving school in North Carolina.

"Once I drove a stock car, I knew it, then and there," Jeff says. "I knew that this was the kind of car I wanted to drive the rest of my career."

Naturally, as soon as Jeff put his mind to it, he became an instant star in a stock car. He joined NASCAR's #2-rated series, where the cars are a bit

Jeff Gordon (No. 24) and Tony Stewart (No. 20)

lighter and not quite as powerful as on the regular circuit. He won 11 races in 1991, and was named rookie of the year.

The next season, Jeff got his first start on NASCAR's main schedule. In 1993, he became a full-time driver on the top circuit. He won his first race in 1994, when he crossed the finish first at the Coca-Cola 600 in Concord, North Carolina.

"The checkered flag came out and I completely lost it," he remembers. "There were tears running down my face."

It was an emotional victory. But it was nothing compared to the joy he felt when he won the first NASCAR Brickyard 400 later that year in Indianapolis. "I don't know if any win will ever top that one," he told the press.

Since then, there have been lots of wins—63 of them by the end of 2003, fourth-best in NASCAR's modern-era rankings. After taking his first season points title in 1995, he won a remarkable 33 races in 96 starts over the next three seasons. He became the youngest winner ever of the famous Daytona 500 in 1997, the year he won his second NASCAR championship. He captured championship titles again in 1998 and in 2001.

All those wins have helped make Jeff one of the most popular drivers in NASCAR history. That popularity not only has helped fuel the spectacular growth of NASCAR throughout the country, but also crossed over to men and women who might not consider themselves racing fans. And through it all, he has remained gracious and humble, open to the media, and accessible to the public.

"I've been blessed with many great opportunities in life," Jeff says. Jeff believes that hard work and determination are the keys to getting past the bumps in the road.

"You can achieve in your life anything that you really set your mind to," he says. "That is not to say that things will always be easy, but you can achieve whatever you really desire to attain."

Now that Jeff is in his thirties, it's no longer correct to call him the "Wonder Boy." In fact, a whole new breed of young stars has emerged on the NASCAR circuit, led by 20-something stars such as Kevin Harvick, Ryan Newman, and Kurt Busch.

But that doesn't mean Gordon is ready to fade from the racing scene, though. In 2003, he won the Virginia 500 and the Subway 500, placed in the top 10 in 20 of his 36 starts, and finished 4th in the points standings—the tenth consecutive season that he finished in the top 10.

In recent years, he also has taken on a new endeavor: car ownership. In 2002, Jeff teamed with Rick Hendrick, the owner of Jeff's No. 24 car, to buy the No. 48 car. Jeff hired an unproven young racer named Jimmie Johnson to drive the 48 car.

Johnson immediately made a big splash at a young age, just like Jeff. He made a run at the NASCAR title in 2002, when he became the first rookie ever to lead the overall points standings. By finishing fifth that year, and second in 2003, Jimmie established himself as a contender for the NASCAR title.

Obviously, Jeff has an eye for talent. No surprise there. It seems that no matter what Jeff does, he's always near the front of the pack.

No. 24, Jeff Gordon

Jeff Gordon: Year by Year

Since taking the checkered flag for the first time at the Coca-Cola 600 in 1994, Jeff has been one of NASCAR's most consistent winners. Here's a season-by-season look at his victory totals:

YEAR	EVENTS	WINS
1992	1	0
1993	30	0
1994	31	2
1995	31	7
1996	31	10
1997	32	10
1998	33	13
1999	34	7
2000	34	3
2001	36	6
2002	36	3
2003	36	2

Jeff Gordon

Dale Earnhardt

Dale Earnhardt Jr.

Kevin Harvick

Jeff Gordon's pit crew

Tire changer at work

2003 NASCAR champion Matt Kenseth celebrates a victory.

Tony Stewart gives the "thumbs up."

Chapter 6

Tony the Tiger

Becoming a star in NASCAR takes talent, desire, and years of hard work. Every driver takes a different path to the top of the charts. Tony Stewart, for instance, made pit stops in just about every kind of car a person can race!

Tony knew that he wanted to be a race-car driver from the time he was a very small boy. In fact, in his book *True Speed*, there's a picture of Tony sitting in a go-kart seat when he was only two months old! Tony first began racing karts when he was seven years old.

Karts are small, low-to-the-ground racing machines with engines that can reach speeds of about 40 miles per hour. For many young racers, this is a great way to get started on the track. Tony and his dad Nelson were dedicated karters for years. Nelson took care of the engines, while Tony kept the machines clean—and did the driving, of course.

By 1983, when he was 12, Tony had won his first

national title, the International Karting Federation Grand National. He won another national title in 1987, and then moved up to more powerful "open-wheel" racing. (Open wheel race cars are the kind of cars seen in the Indy 500 and Formula 1 races.)

To this day, Tony credits his dad for helping him become a success on the track. "He never let me settle for second. If he saw that I wasn't giving 100 percent, then he was on me pretty hard about it. He pushed me to be better. He never pressured me to be the best in the world, just to be the best driver I could be."

When he wasn't racing, Tony was a regular kid. He was nuts for radio-controlled cars (and he says he still is), played trombone in the high school marching band, and played basketball with his friends. But he knew these were just hobbies. He was a race car driver and he knew that was his destiny.

In 1991, Tony started racing "TQs," which stands for three-quarter midgets. They're like smaller versions of open-wheel racing machines that run on major international tracks. In TQs, Tony excelled quickly. By 1994, he was the national champion. Before long, being a national champion was something Tony would have to get used to.

In 1995, Tony took part in three different national

Tony Stewart prepares to race.

racing circuits. Well, he actually did more than take part—he won them all! Tony became the first (and only) driver to win the U.S. Auto Club's National Midget, Sprint, and Silver Crown series championships. He competed in 59 races in all, often driving in two races in one weekend.

Tony kept trying new ways to race, and in 1996, he drove in some NASCAR circuit races in stock cars for the first time. He also began driving in the Indy Racing League, which featured very powerful open-wheel cars. He was the IRL rookie of the year in 1996 and kept his national-champion streak going, winning the IRL overall title in 1997.

Tony, an Indiana native, had grown up dreaming of racing in the famed Indy 500 event. However, the power and lure of NASCAR was calling him to switch gears once again. Tony knew that NASCAR was the top of the racing world, and it would be the place to test his skills to the utmost. Several car owners wanted Tony to bring his driving talents to NASCAR full-time. Former Super Bowl-champion NFL coach Joe Gibbs made the best arguments, and Tony joined Gibbs' team in 1998. Making the jump was a big decision for Tony.

"The biggest reservation I had was that a lot of

people suggested that none of the racing I had done before had prepared me for [NASCAR's top division]. In a lot of ways, they were right, because it's unlike anything else in the world. But they hadn't considered this: I had learned how to win!"

Joe Gibbs certainly knew how to spot winners. (He led football's Washington Redskins to three Super Bowl titles.) He knew Tony had a great future. But not even Gibbs guessed just how quickly his new driver would succeed. "None of us dreamed he'd win a race," Gibbs said. "We thought he'd be up close. None of us dreamed he'd even be in the top 10."

Tony kicked off his 1999 rookie season with a bang by grabbing the second spot on the starting grid of the Daytona 500. Though he finished that race in 28th place, he had caught everyone's eye. He was often among the leaders as the season progressed, and he was a rare rookie in the top 10 in the points standings. In September, Tony became the first rookie since 1987 to win a race, capturing the 500-mile event at Richmond.

He topped that feat by winning two more races, which set a record for wins by a rookie. He wound up fourth overall in points, the first rookie in NASCAR history to finish in the top 5. He had 12 top-5 finishes in races, 21 top-10s, and won more than $2.5 million. It was truly a rookie season to remember.

For Tony, however, it was only the beginning. In 2000, he doubled his victory total to six, breaking Dale Earnhardt Sr.'s record for wins by a second-year driver. In 2001, Tony finished second overall behind Jeff Gordon in the NASCAR standings.

In 2002, Tony and most of the NASCAR community knew that he had a good chance to capture the title. Tony had a great summer, winning three races and often finishing in the top five 15 times. He and his team worked hard on consistency—doing well every week, instead of winning one week and not finishing the next. They took over the top spot in the standings in September and never looked back.

Heading into the final race of the 2002 season at Miami's Homestead track in November, Tony led veteran driver Mark Martin in the season championship chase by only 89 points. If Martin won the race, Tony had to finish at least twenty-second to guarantee himself the NASCAR title. Homestead was a tough race, and engine troubles plagued Tony and his team. But at the end, he finished in eighteenth place, while Martin managed only fourth.

Tony Stewart was a champion again, this time the

Tony Stewart

top driver in the top racing circuit in the country. The kid who had started out in karts, moved up to midgets, and dabbled in Indy cars had driven right to the top in only his third season on NASCAR's top level.

Tony remains one of the top stock car drivers in the world, with a passion for winning and doing his best. He has a reputation for being a bit intense, but he believes that intensity is what has made him great.

"Everybody likes to win," he writes. "I'm no different. But I guess I'd have to say this: I'm not a good loser." Fortunately for Tony, he hasn't had to worry about that too often.

Double Duty

In one day, Tony Stewart drove from New York City to Kansas City, Missouri! Well, not really, but he did race that distance of about 1,100 miles. Twice in his career, Tony has pulled off an amazing two-race day, competing in the Indy 500 and then the Coca-Cola 600. It's an amazing feat when you consider that the two races are held in different states in different types of cars!

In 1999, Tony's rookie season, he and his team decided to try to give "Double Duty" a shot. His busy day started in Indianapolis, where the big race started just before noon on May 30. He zoomed around the famous Indianapolis Motor Speedway in his open-wheel car and finished ninth, with a time of just over three hours.

That race was over, but Tony just kept moving fast, hopping into a helicopter on the Indy infield and flying to a nearby airport. There he boarded a private jet sent for him by Home Depot, his NASCAR sponsor. While flying from Indianapolis to Charlotte, North Carolina, Tony caught a quick nap, had some food, and prepared to race…again!

In Charlotte, he hopped into another helicopter and landed at the Charlotte Motor Speedway. Since he had missed the prerace drivers' meeting while flying, Tony had to start this night-time race in last (43rd) place at 6:15 PM. But even though he had already driven 500 miles that day, he zoomed toward the front of the pack and finished 4th in the 600. He was dog-tired, but it was a thrilling day for Tony and his fans.

In 2001, he repeated the grueling feat, this time raising nearly $250,000 for a children's charity. Joe Gibbs, Tony, and others donated money for every lap Tony finished—and he ended up finishing them all! Tony's "Double Duty" trips took endurance, great timing, a little help, and lots of driving skill.

82

Chapter 7

Marvelous Matt

When you think of the state of Wisconsin, you don't normally think of stock car racing. Cheese, maybe, or the Green Bay Packers football team. But actually this northern Midwestern state has a long history with stock car racing, and several popular circuits are run all over the state. From this tradition of great driving came a young man who fulfilled his great potential in 2003.

From the time he was a youngster growing up in Cambridge, Wisconsin, Matt had loved anything with wheels and a motor. He toyed around on his dad's lawn mower, played with slot cars, and worked on his BMX bike. When Matt was 13, his dad made a deal with him. If Matt would help clean and care for a racing sports car, he could drive it when he turned 16. Matt kept up his part of the deal, and not long after that important birthday, he found himself not just behind the wheel, but under the checkered flag. Matt was a racing phenomenon, winning many races at tracks all over Wisconsin against drivers twice his age.

While he was driving, he was still going to high school. After class, he added to his automotive knowledge by working at a car parts store, sometimes also working on engines and car bodies. By the time he was 19, he had become the youngest race series winner in state history, and had also won several track championships. By 1996, Matt had won just about everything he could win in the Midwest and he set his sights higher.

Matt's first taste of big-time stock car racing came in a race in 1996. Though he finished 31st, it whetted his appetite for more. However, few rides were on the horizon for the young driver…until an old friend from Wisconsin changed Matt's life.

Robbie Reiser had been a fellow competitor on those small Midwestern tracks, and he remembered Matt when he was trying to find a driver for one of his race cars. In 1997, Matt and Robbie started a professional partnership that remains one of the tightest twosomes on the NASCAR circuit. Robbie was the crew chief and Matt was the driver. By the end of that first year, they had racked up enough high finishes for Matt to come in second in the voting for

Matt Kenseth

the rookie of the year award.

In 1998, even though they had problems lining up a sponsor, Matt and Robbie captured their first NASCAR circuit victory, a 200-mile race in Rockingham, North Carolina. By the end of the season, Matt had ended up in second place overall, with three wins and 17 top-five finishes. During that season, Matt reached another career milestone by earning his first ride in a car on the highest NASCAR level. He was filling in for Bill Elliott, and all he did was post the highest finish (sixth) for a driver in his first top-level race since 1980! In 1999, Matt again nearly won NASCAR's #2-rated series, finishing only 26 points behind Dale Earnhardt Jr.

NASCAR veterans were beginning to pay attention to the youngster. "Matt is a superstar in the making," said veteran Mark Martin. "If you were going to build a race-car driver from scratch, he'd be the one [to do it]."

An important part of Matt's success on the track was due to the DeWalt Power Tools pit crew assembled by Reiser. Each year, NASCAR pit crews take part in a special competition to see who is the best and the fastest at changing tires, gassing up, and servicing a car. Matt's crew has twice captured this important contest, setting a world record for fastest four-tire,

Matt Kenseth fastens his helmet before a race.

full-fuel pit stops (less than 14 seconds!). Matt's winning ways on the track carried over to the crew, and they know that the only way to make it to the top in NASCAR is as a team.

That team made the leap to NASCAR's top level full-time in 2000. The biggest moment of that year came when Matt became the first rookie ever to win the important Coca-Cola 600 at Charlotte (N.C.) Motor Speedway. Matt kept up his high finishes (he had 11 top 10s),
and at the end of the year, he surprised some when he was named rookie of the year over Dale Earnhardt Jr.

In 2001, Matt didn't have as much success, but he bounced back in 2002 to lead the series with five wins, finishing eighth overall. He was poised for greatness, and in 2003, he delivered.

Matt won the third race of the 2003 season, the UAW DaimlerChrysler 400 in Las Vegas. Over the course of the next dozen races, Matt finished out of the top 10 only once. He just kept up the pressure on individual race leaders, and by mid-summer had a commanding lead in the season points race. High finishes week after week are a better way to capture a season title than occasional bursts of victory, and Matt was on the right track.

In the next-to-last race of the season, Matt finished fourth. That was good enough to clinch the NASCAR season title. Matt and his team celebrated joyously. He received the NASCAR championship trophy and a check for $4.25 million after the final race of the season in Miami. The trophy would head home with Matt to Wisconsin. Who knows how many more times Matt and the championship trophy will make that trip?

Matt's Marks

On his way to the 2003 NASCAR title, Matt and his team looked to consistency and high finishes to rack up the points. Matt won the third race of the season in Las Vegas to take the lead for the first time. In his next 12 races he finished in the top 10 eleven times.

2003 Results

Races	36	Victories	1
Points	5,022	Top 5 finishes	25
Overall finish	1st		

Chase for the Championship

How does a driver win the NASCAR NEXTEL Cup Series title? He needs a fast car, a great team…and a calculator!

In each race, the winning driver in each race gets 180 points. The next five finishers (second through sixth) receive five points less in descending order (170, 165, 160, etc.) Positions seven through 11 are separated by four points (146, 142, etc.), while the rest of the field is separated by three points (123, 120, 117, etc.). Even finishing last (in 43rd place) earns a driver 34 points. In addition, bonus points are added for each lap led and leading the most laps. After each race, a driver's points are totaled up and added to his season total.

In 2004, things change after the 26th race of the season. The top 10 drivers (and any others within 400 points of the leader) go into a special pool. Their points are adjusted so that the leader has only a five-point margin over the rest of the field. Over the final 10 races, these drivers take part in the exciting "Chase for the Championship." There might be a new leader every week until the season finale in Miami. Tthe driver with the most points after the final race on November 21 will be the NASCAR NEXTEL Cup Series champion.

82

Chapter 8

Young... and Fast!

The list of great drivers in NASCAR history is long and filled with legendary names: Petty, Earnhardt, Yarborough, Gordon, and more. Recent champions like Tony Stewart and Matt Kenseth have taken big steps toward becoming legends themselves.

In the late 1990s and early 2000s, several new drivers joined NASCAR's top circuit, bringing a wave of new talent into the series. They came from a wide variety of backgrounds, but they all brought a powerful need to do two things: Go fast and win! Here's a quick look at some future legends.

It can be hard to follow in any father's footsteps, but few sons have tried to fill such big shoes as the ones Dale Earnhardt Jr., stepped into. "Junior," as he is known, is the son of the famous "Man in Black," Dale Earnhardt, who won a record-tying seven NASCAR driving titles. Not only that, but Dale Jr.'s grandfather Ralph had been a hard-driving NASCAR pioneer.

So it was no surprise that Dale Jr. had been around cars his whole life.

After several years in smaller series, by the time he was 21, Dale Jr. had worked his way up to the NASCAR's #2-rated series. Two years later, he was that circuit's season champ. He followed that up with another in 1999. It was time to take the big leap and join his dad on the biggest stage of them all. In 2000, he took a full-time ride in a car bearing the number 8: a number his grandfather had made famous more than 50 years earlier. Junior (also called "Little E") won twice in his first season, carrying on a great family tradition. Dale Jr. has become one of the most popular drivers in NASCAR, as well as one of its best.

In 2001, Kevin Harvick had one of the best rookie seasons in NASCAR history, and he has gotten even better since. Kevin grew up in a racing family and he got his first kart when he graduated kindergarten! By the time he was 10, he was a national champion and went on to win six more national titles.

Kevin moved up to stock cars in 1992 and made the big jump to NASCAR's #2-rated series in 2000, where he was named rookie of the year. In 2001, he expected to spend another year learning the ropes in lower-level races, but he was tapped by team owner

Dale Earnhardt Jr.

Richard Childress to make the jump to NASCAR's "big leagues." In an amazing year that saw him compete in 69 races (the only driver ever to put in a full season in both of NASCAR's top circuits), Kevin won in his third start, had six top-5 finishes, and 16 top-10s.

It was no big surprise that he was rookie of the year in that division, too. He has continued his success, racking up nine wins through 2003, a season in which he finished second in the points race.

Jimmie Johnson started his NASCAR career with a bang, becoming the first rookie ever to win the pole at the Daytona 500 in 2002. It was a fast track to the top for the former motorcycle and off-road racer. He was tapped by Jeff Gordon to join his team after only two years on NASCAR's lower-level circuit. Jimmie was a rare Californian in a "Southern" sport, but he soon fit right in. Having a boss and teacher like Gordon, a four-time champ, didn't hurt, either.

"At first it was intimidating," Jimmie remembers. "I went from watching Jeff race on TV to having him as my boss and teammate. He was a tremendous help to me that first season, teaching me about life on and off the track."

On the track, Jimmie didn't need much coaching. They just put him in the No. 48 car and watched him

Jimmie Johnson

go. He won his first race in April, 2002, at the California Speedway in front of friends and family. He also won two races at Dover, Delaware.

In late September, he reached another milestone. With a 10th-place finish at the race in Kansas, he became the first rookie ever to lead the season point standings. Jimmie's 5th-place finish marked him as a racer to watch, and he kept it up in 2003, racking up three race wins and a 2nd-place overall finish.

Ryan Newman burst on the scene in 2002 and almost matched Johnson—rookie record for rookie record. Ryan had joined NASCAR's top series after two years in NASCAR's #2-rated series and after earning an engineering degree from Purdue University. Ryan's knowledge of automotive science gives him an edge in the garage, while his go-for-the-front speed makes him a force on the track.

Beginning in July, 2002, Ryan was in the top 5 in eight out of ten races, earning his first win at the New Hampshire 300. He won six pole positions during the season and racked up 22 top-10 finishes. Those 22 finishes were good enough to put him in a tie for first in top-10 finishes. His outstanding season earned him rookie of the year honors. In 2003, he did even better, finishing sixth overall in the standings. He won

Ryan Newman

a season-high 8 races, including six races in a 13-week period beginning with the Tropicana 400 in mid-July.

Though he has not won an overall championship yet, Kurt Busch is showing that he has the stuff to win it all. Kurt was only 23 years old when he won the first race of his career, the Food City 500 in 2002. Two months from the end of the season, he stood 12th on the points list—a good showing, but he would go on to do even better. Kurt won three of the last five races in 2002, including back-to-back victories in the Old Dominion 500 and the Napa 500. Then Kurt won twice more in the early part of 2003. So, over the course of 15 events, he drove his Ford Taurus to Victory Lane five times. Kurt's strong finish in 2002 vaulted him to 3rd in the points standings. He went on to win four races in 2003 to place 11th.

All these young drivers are continuing a tradition of more than a half century of outstanding speedway superstars. From the early days of dirt tracks and family cars to today's high-tech ovals and supercharged stock cars, NASCAR has come a long way. Leading the pack, then and now, is a group of drivers who combine talent, courage, and skill to zoom toward one goal: the checkered flag at the finish line.

Kurt Busch

In the Pits

NASCAR racers know that it's not just the driver who wins races, it's the team. During every race, drivers will head to the pits 8 to 12 times. Even a slight delay during one of those trips can mean the difference between a checkered flag and a place back in the pack.

Early NASCAR racers didn't pay much attention to pit crews. They would just use local mechanics or volunteers at each race. In the 1960s, the Wood Brothers team changed all that. By using one team for all races and giving each person a specific job, they revolutionized pit stops.

Today, NASCAR rules say that seven team members can go "over the wall" during a pit stop. In less than 17 or 18 seconds, a top team can change four tires, put in 22 gallons of fuel, give water to the driver, clean a windshield, and then clear out!

The seven pit crew members are:

• One jack man. He slides a large jack under one side of the car and with a powerful pump, raises the

82

car so one pair of tires is off the ground. After two tires are changed, he does the same for the other side.

• Two tire changers (front and rear) use air guns on long rubber hoses to take off the five lug nuts that hold the tires on the car.

• Two tire carriers (front and rear) carry the 80-pound tires to the car and "hang" them on the lug nuts. Then they take the old tires to the wall for disposal.

• One catch-can man uses a special tool to open a vent at the back of the car to allow fuel to be poured in and catch any overflow gas.

• One gas man, who carries the 11-gallon fuel can and pours gas into car.

Dale Earnhardt Jr.'s pit crew hurries to get him back in the race.

Kurt Busch's pit crew fuels up his car.

All Time Winners

In this book, you've met many of the greatest drivers in NASCAR history. Their success on the track can be most easily measured by how often they won. Here is a list (through 2003) of the top 15 race winners in NASCAR history.

DRIVER	RACES WON
Richard Petty	200
David Pearson	105
Bobby Allison	84
Darrell Waltrip	84
Cale Yarborough	83
Dale Earnhardt Sr.	76
Jeff Gordon	64
Rusty Wallace	54
Lee Petty	54
Ned Jarrett	50
Herb Thomas	49
Buck Baker	46
Bill Elliott	43
Junior Johnson	40
Tim Flock	40

Speeds can exceed 180 mph in a NASCAR race!

Glossary

backstretch The long, straight area of a track opposite the finish line stretch.

banks The steep, slanted corners of speedways. The banking helps drivers keep up their speed through turns.

checkered flag Black-and-white checkered flag waved when the winner of a race crosses the finish line.

crew chief The leader of the race team on the track. He is in charge of the pit crew and is also lead strategist working with driver via radio link.

engineering The study of machines and energy and how things work.

go-kart A small racing machine with a low-power engine. Built low to the ground, they can be driven by young children.

green flag Waved to signify the start of a race.

lap One trip around a track as measured from one starting spot.

NASCAR National Association for Stock Car Auto Racing

open-wheel   A type of racing. Open-wheel cars are long and slender and the wheels are not enclosed by the car's body, unlike stock cars.

pit crews   Seven race-team members who service the race car during periodic stops during a race.

pole position   The best starting position in a race, in the front row nearest the inside of the track.

sponsors   Companies that give money to support a driver's team in return for the team advertising the companies' products.

superspeedway   Any racetrack longer than a mile, but usually referring to 1.5- to 2.5-mile long tracks—all with high banked curves and corners.

TQs   Nickname for "three-quarters," a type of scaled-down open-wheel racing often done by younger drivers.

victory lane   The place on the pit road where the winner of a race drives his car to receive his trophy and winnings.

NASCAR Champs

Dale Earnhardt is tied for the most titles ever at NASCAR's highest level. Here is a ranking of drivers with the most championships:

Richard Petty	7	David Pearson	3
Dale Earnhardt	7	Cale Yarborough	3
Jeff Gordon	4	Darrell Waltrip	3
Lee Petty	3		

Plus, these drivers won two championships:

Tim Flock	Ned Jarrett
Buck Baker	Terry Labonte
Joe Weatherly	Herb Thomas

Superstars of Tomorrow

Where will the next Pettys, Earnhardts, Stewarts, and Kenseths come from? Scouts for the top racing teams are always on the lookout for young talent. They scout other NASCAR regional series, truck races, sports car races, even off-road races. Team owners know that the best drivers will be able to race in any vehicle; the trick is finding ones who will win!

Brian Vickers is one of the brightest young stars on NASCAR's top circuit. Though he is only 20, he has already put in two full seasons in NASCAR's #2-rated series, collecting several wins and more than 15 top-10 finishes. "There's no doubt in my mind that Brian is going to have a long and productive career," says team owner Rick Hendrick.

Racing up behind Brian is 18-year-old Kyle Busch, the younger brother of Kurt Busch. Kyle started out in ARCA sports car races, and jumped into a seat in NASCAR's #2-rated series as soon as he turned 18 in 2003. Kyle might be the next young driver to make the jump to the top level.

"A race car doesn't know how old the driver is," NASCAR veteran Michael Waltrip says.

82

A Driver's Day

Today's NASCAR drivers all have their own mental approaches to race day. But all of them follow pretty much the same procedure. If you were a NASCAR driver, here is what the hours of your race day might be like:

8 A.M.   Wake up, eat breakfast with your family in the motor home parked on the track's infield. Most drivers fly to each race, then stay in a motor home for easy access to the track and pit area.

9–10 A.M.   Meet with sponsors, team members, and fans.

10–11 A.M.   Meet with crew chief about final thoughts on race strategy; check weather and track conditions.

11–11:30 A.M.   Attend mandatory drivers' meeting, where all drivers meet with NASCAR and track officials, go over race rules, schedules, and times.

11:30–12:00 Attend chapel service, popular with many drivers.

12:00 Time for some lunch and a final trip to the bathroom.

12:30 P.M. Standing by your car or riding in the back of a convertible, you and the other drivers are introduced to the crowd one by one in order of starting position. You all put on helmets and safety harnesses. The cars are rolled or pushed out to the starting grid, where you and the other drivers rev up your engines.

1:00 P.M. When the track is clear, the pace car starts out slowly, leading the cars around the track. As you pass under the green flag, you and the other drivers hit the gas and the race is on!

PHOTOGRAPHY CREDITS